Would You Believe...

Mexico, people picnic at granny's grave?

and other dynastic delights

Richard Platt

OXFORD
UNIVERSITY PRESS

OXFORD
UNIVERSITY PRESS

Great Clarendon Street, Oxford OX2 6DP

Oxford University Press is a department of the University of Oxford. It furthers the University's objective of excellence in research, scholarship, and education by publishing worldwide in

Oxford   New York

Auckland   Cape Town   Dar es Salaam
Hong Kong   Karachi   Kuala Lumpur   Madrid
Melbourne   Mexico City   Nairobi   New Delhi
Shanghai   Taipei   Toronto

With offices in

Argentina   Austria   Brazil   Chile
Czech Republic   France   Greece   Guatemala
Hungary   Italy   Japan   Poland   Portugal
Singapore   South Korea   Switzerland   Thailand
Turkey   Ukraine   Vietnam

Oxford is a registered trade mark of Oxford University Press in the UK and in certain other countries

Text copyright © Oxford University Press 2010

The moral rights of the author have been asserted

Database right Oxford University Press (maker)

First published 2010

British Library Cataloguing in Publication Data
Data available

ISBN 978-0-19-911985-1

1 3 5 7 9 10 8 6 4 2

Originated by Oxford University Press

Created by BOOKWORK Ltd

Printed in China

WARNING: *The practices in this book are for information only and should not be tried at home!*

Contents

Introduction

FAMILIES! THERE'S NOTHING else quite like 'em is there? You just can't beat the warmth of a family welcome or the generosity of relations when you get into a fix.
But ... you can also rely on parents, brothers and sisters to say ruder, crueller things to you than anyone else would dare.

What exactly is a family, though? For many of us it's the "nuclear" family. This isn't a war weapon – though sometimes it may feel like it. It's the traditional group of Mum, Dad and their children.

A family can be more or less than this. A single mum and her daughter make a family of two. And for an orphaned boy living on the street, "family" means the gang that protects him and shares everything with him. This book looks at all kinds of families: how they start and end; how they work and how they don't; who runs them, and how relations are – well – related. If you think you know all about families, you may be in for some surprises.

Would You Believe ... ?

Who, what, when and why?
Who called a wolf "Mum"? What's the most common family name? When was a gaol the most popular place to marry? Why did families in Ancient Rome leave daughters out in the cold? If you want to know the answers, turn the page.

Steps and Halves
and Singles

HEY! WHAT'S SO NORMAL about parents who stick together? You're hardly unusual if you have a stepmother or stepfather because your parents have moved on and married again. Out of every six kids, at least one has a parent who wasn't around when they were born.

Remixed families are more common than ever. They can get complicated, but working out who is a step or a half is easy. Half-brothers and sisters have the same mum *or* the same dad. Steps share neither.

Steps to Hollywood ▲
Veteran Hollywood actor Mickey Rooney has created a step-family to end them all. Married eight times, he has nine children. He's shown here with three children from his third marriage. His oldest son Mickey has six stepmothers.

Drama queens and kings
Step-families from the past have been famous for falling out, and authors and playwrights love the drama this creates. They use "wicked" stepfathers or mothers to prop up their plots.

HAMLET

Steps in fiction ▲ ▶
Writers use the feuds of step-families to create characters audiences love to hate. The traditional tales of Snow White (above) and Cinderella rely on wicked stepmothers. In his play *Hamlet* (right), William Shakespeare made his hero's uncle and mother marry to create a deadly stepfather.

Shaking up the family

Step-parents and their children come as a package. You don't get to choose them, nor do you have a lifetime to get used to their habits. So some are bound to spice up family life when they arrive.

The bad picture sometimes painted of step-parents in fiction is a cruel step-lie. Research shows that step-kids are just as happy and successful as those from regular families, and often better off than children whose parents fell out but stayed together.

Catherine of Aragon

Anne Boleyn

Jane Seymour

Anne of Cleeves

Catherine Howard

Katherine Parr

Mary I

Elizabeth I

Edward VI

All those steps ▲
Desperate to have a son, English king Henry VIII built a fiendishly complicated web of steps. His first daughter Mary (later queen) had a total of five stepmothers. One died, one had her marriage to the king annulled and two were executed. When Mary died, her half-sister Elizabeth became Queen.

Would You Believe . . . ? Would You Believe . . . ?

Frosty families
In traditional Greenland Inuit society, steps and halves had little meaning. Single women with children simply found a husband, who became Dad. Men commonly lent and borrowed their wives, and a woman's current husband was the father of all her kids.

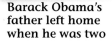
Barack Obama's father left home when he was two

One's enough
One happy parent is better than the complete set, fighting. Single-parent families are even more common than steps – one in four children lives with one parent. With so many solo mums, it's not surprising that some of their kids grow up to be famous names. Even the US president Barack Obama was raised without a dad.

◀ **Just us and Mum**
More and more women raise their kids alone, not because they have to, but because they prefer to. Often well educated and well off, they reckon they can make a better job of bringing up their children without help from Dad.

Let's get Hitched!

HALF OF US DON'T bother with it, some of us spend a fortune on it and many of us put it off until our kids are old enough to enjoy the party. Getting married ties two lives together with an ancient promise – even though the modern ceremony can be distinctly wacky.

● ● ● ● ● ● ● ● ● ● ● ●

Marriage began not with rings and beautiful dresses, but with kidnapping: a man simply captured the woman he wanted, often from another tribe. Later, men bought or traded wives.

▲ Medieval marriage
Luxury laws in the Middle Ages (500–1500 CE) kept wedding clothes simple. To stop wasteful extravagance, couples could not marry in clothes trimmed with jewels or gold – unless they earned 251 marks (£1.2 million) a year.

Arranged marriage ▶
When Louis, Duke of Burgundy (in France) got married in 1797, he was claiming a prize. His 11-year-old bride, Maria-Adélaïde of Savoy (also now part of France), had been promised to him the year before as part of a deal that ended a nine-year-long war.

▲ Married in gaol
Eighteenth-century London men whose parents disapproved of their choice of bride could marry secretly – in prison! For a small fee, vicars locked up for debts in Fleet gaol married couples in the chapel. A new law banned these Fleet marriages in 1753.

Proof of a wedding ▼
Marriage certificates began as special licences in the Middle Ages. They allowed a couple to marry instantly – and secretly. Without one, marriages had to be announced publicly three weeks in advance.

◄ Ancient pre-nup
Like a pre-nuptial (before marriage) agreement between celebrities today, a Jewish Ketubah is a legal contract. It promises the wife food and clothing and a fee if the marriage ends in divorce.

◄ **Marriage certificate, 1833**

Illegitimacy
Today nobody asks whether your parents are married or not. For many people, being illegitimate (born outside marriage) doesn't matter. But in the past, the facts of your birth were very important. Illegitimate children were called bastards and could not inherit family wealth.

Would You Believe . . . ? Would You Believe . . . ?

Wedding finger
We wear a wedding ring on the fourth finger of our left hand because of an ancient (and incorrect) belief that a special vein runs from there directly to our heart. Or perhaps it's because rings wear down slowly on this little-used finger!

Wedding history
Many wedding traditions, such as special clothes and vows, come from Ancient Rome. But in the past, few people married for love. The rich arranged marriages to unite families. The poor just moved in together.

▲ **William I**
Illegitimacy was no problem for William of Normandy (now part of France). He became duke on the death of his father, who never married his mother, an undertaker's daughter. Nicknamed "William the Bastard" by his countrymen, he conquered England in 1066 and became King William I.

When brides were sold, the "wed" was the sum a groom paid for his wife

Jumping the broom ▶
Not all traditional weddings were official ceremonies. Welsh gypsies and slaves on American plantations married by jumping over a broom. Today, many African Americans add this ritual to the end of their weddings.

In White or under Water

▲ Royal regalia
Kings and queens set wedding styles. Queen Victoria's choice of a white dress made white weddings hugely popular. When her great, great, great grandson, Prince Charles, married in 1981, British brides copied the style of the famous dress of his bride Diana.

AN ORGAN PLAYS AND A WHITE dress with a bride inside drifts into the church. It sounds traditional, but white weddings with flowers and bridesmaids began only in the 19th century. Outside European and American Churches, traditional weddings have taken many forms, some much more colourful.

• • • • • • • • • • • • • • • • • • • •

What is perhaps surprising is how many different peoples share similar marriage customs. Wedding cakes, for example, were as popular among the Iroquois Native American people as they were among people in Ancient Rome.

Would You Believe . . . ?

Tree marriage
Among people of India's Brahmin caste (class), older brothers were supposed to marry before younger ones. If a younger brother found a wife first, his older brother married a tree in a ceremony that stopped tradition from obstructing love.

▼ Massive marriages
Fancy a big wedding? How about saying "I do" with 2,074 other couples? South Korean minister Sun Myung Moon of the Unification Church blessed the marriages of this vast crowd in New York's Madison Square Garden in 1982.

Rice and shoes

Wedding customs aim to bring good luck, and many are popular world-wide. Throwing rice or grain is a sign that the couple will never be hungry. Shoes show wealth (the poor go barefoot) so guests tie them to newlyweds' cars.

◄ **Bedouin wedding**
Among the Bedouin desert dwellers of north Africa and the Middle East, weddings such as this one from 1938, traditionally lasted a week. At the end, a camel carried the bride to the groom's tent.

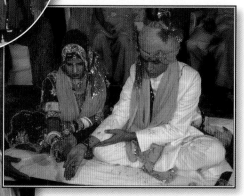

▲ **Hindu wedding**
There is no "standard' Hindu wedding, like a Christian wedding, but all kinds are glittering and glamorous. Brides of the Rajput clans wear dresses of brilliant orange, red, yellow, pink or green, and are decked out in gold and jewels.

Today, people marry in all kinds of wacky ways. But you can be sure that when their feet are on dry land again, they will follow the rituals and superstitions that were used to bring good fortune to countless couples before them.

▲ **Salty marriage**
In Britain, weddings must take place in a church, a government register office or another officially approved place. Elsewhere in the world, laws are less strict. Even skydiving and SCUBA weddings are almost normal – although kissing is tricky!

Wedding customs around the world make the European white wedding look very boring

Growing
up in Style

▲ Boys in skirts
Until about 1900, European toddlers wore dresses. Boys celebrated the end of infancy by wearing breeches (trousers) for the first time. Here 17th-century French king Louis XIV stands next to his unbreeched brother.

C HANGING FROM A CHILD TO AN adult is something celebrated today with a party or a dance. But would you look forward to your "coming of age" ritual so much if it involved hunger and thirst, torture or mutilation? Some traditional manhood ceremonies around the world may seem cruel, but they tested bravery, strength and endurance at times when these qualities mattered more than they do today.

● ● ● ● ● ● ● ● ● ● ● ● ● ●

Native American boys of the Plains had to endure starvation and loneliness as part of their vision quest (opposite). But as adults they would face hardship and danger. Hunger and death would be familiar companions to them.

Whether dangerous and scary or tame and familiar, growing-up rituals help us to move into adulthood

◄ Bar Mitzvah
Religious people celebrate their children growing up by encouraging them to take a fuller part in worship. Catholic Christians celebrate First Communion. Jewish boys celebrate Bar Mitzvah and girls Bat Mitzvah when they read aloud from the Torah (Jewish holy book) for the first time.

Rituals today

Celebrations of growing up today are happy affairs, though perhaps less character-forming than vision quests. But brutal adulthood rituals haven't entirely disappeared. They survive secretly and illegally as "hazing" or initiation ceremonies of clubs, gangs and army schools.

Egyptian princess Neferure (with her tutor) wearing a sidelock

Would You Believe . . . . ?

Scary plunge
Some growing-up rituals can be terrifying. On Pentecost Island in the Pacific Ocean, boys become men only when they have stripped naked and hurled themselves from a 30m (98ft) tower. Only a jungle vine tied to their feet stops them dashing their head on the ground.

▲ Vision quest

This Sioux shaman (spirit-priest) is recalling his vision quest. For a Native American boy of the Plains, a vision quest was a journey of self-discovery. For up to four days, he would sit alone, fasting and thirsty. The spirits who visited him at this time gave him lasting wisdom.

First hair cut ▲

Many families around the world celebrate a baby's first haircut, usually between the ages of one and three. But in Ancient Egypt, a haircut marked the end of childhood. Children wore their hair plaited in a sidelock and rejoiced when their hair was cropped at around 14 years old.

▼ High-school prom

For most of us, adulthood begins when school ends, so scholars everywhere celebrate when they graduate. Widely imitated elsewhere, the American high-school prom is a formal ball. The bright and beautiful get to show off, but some kids and parents dismiss it as a costly fashion show.

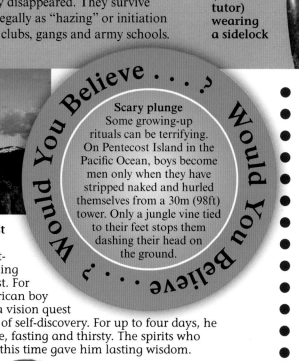

Born to Rule
just like Dad

TODAY WE KNOW THAT everyone is born equal, but in the past, noble families believed they were better than others. They used their wealth and power to ensure their children were rich and powerful too. Called dynasties, these "well-bred", privileged families ruled nations for centuries.

● ●

Dynasties often used religion to claim power, saying that God made them great. Their downtrodden citizens disagreed, and by the 20th century, revolutions had removed most dynasties. A few still rule nations.

Would You Believe . . . ?

Blue blood
Today we joke that posh people have blue blood. The idea began among 13th-century Spanish nobles. Spain's oldest families were proud of their pale skin. Seen through it, veins looked blue. Work in the sun tanned common people's skin, hiding the veins.

▲ Rameses II (mummy)

Pharaohs ▲ ▶
Ancient Egyptians believed their pharaohs (kings) were gods. This belief allowed just 30 dynasties to rule the country for 3,000 years. Rameses and Nefertari were from the 19th.

▲ Queen Nefertari, wife of Rameses II (13th century BCE)

Tang polo ▲
China's dynasties mostly ended in wars, as one ruling family replaced another. The dynasties were named. This figurine of a woman playing polo is from the Tang dynasty (7th–10th centuries). Chinese emperors lived in a golden world of privilege, separate from the people they ruled, and unseen by them.

◀ Coat of 719 arms
Europe's nobles were proud of their ancestry and when they married they combined their family crests by quartering (dividing into four). For a few generations, this was sensible, but repeated quartering produced a patchwork of badges; like this one made for the Marquess of Chandos in the 1880s.

Quartered coat ▶
of arms

Family bird ▲
This black eagle was the crest of the Romanov dynasty that ruled Russia for three centuries. The last tsar (emperor), Nicholas, wore a fur cloak decorated with pearls the size of marbles while his people starved. By 1917, they had had enough, and revolutionaries shot the whole family.

17th-century tsar Peter the Great put into his wife's bedroom the pickled head of a man who flirted with her

Bad or mad?

Royal and noble families want us to think that they are not just rich, but somehow different from ordinary people. However, their behaviour reveals the truth – they can be just as wicked, dishonest, immoral and generally bad as anyone else.

Outrageous nobles ▼
The Hervey family scandalized Britain for six generations. In the 18th century, Bess (below) lived for 25 years with her lover, the Duke of Devonshire, and his wife. Some 200 years later, Fred Hervey, the 7th Marquess of Bristol, was a jewel thief and squandered the family fortune of £35 million.

▲ **Elizabeth Hervey**

◀ **4th Earl Ferrers**

▲ **Killer aristocrat**
Laurence Shirley lived a wild life in Paris before becoming 4th Earl Ferrers in 1745. Famously bad-tempered, he stabbed a servant over a bad oyster. When he shot another, he became the last English lord to be executed for murder.

Finding a new Family

▲ **Foundlings**
Children found abandoned were called foundlings. Those not adopted were cared for in foundling hospitals, like this one in the USA in the early 20th century.

IF YOU'VE EVER WANTED SOMETHING you know you can't have, you'll understand the special magic of adoption. It creates families for couples who can't have children of their own. It makes sure that kids whose birth parents can't raise them grow up in loving, caring families. However, adoption wasn't always like this. It has a dodgy history of slavery, baby sales and wolf-mothers!

In Ancient Rome, 20 centuries ago, reluctant mums left babies by the roadside. Passers-by adopted them, but often sold them as slaves. In 17th-century America, farmers bought unwanted children from England and put them to work as "indentured servants".

Would You Believe . . . ?

Fostering saga
Viking families exchanged children, fostering those of another family to strengthen friendships. Parents could be closer to foster children than to their own. One mother carved on her foster son's grave, "It's better to leave a good foster son than a bad son."

Romulus and Remus ▶
According to a Roman legend, twins Romulus and Remus were found abandoned in a basket by a she-wolf, who adopted and raised them. As adults, the twins built the city of Rome.

▼ **Adopted by a star**
Europe and the USA have tough
adoption laws, so some people
adopt in countries where rules are
not as strict. Critics accuse them
of taking advantage of birth-
parents' poverty, but supporters
say the adopted children will be
healthier, wealthier and happier.

**Madonna with
her adopted
son David
Banda, in
Malawi**

▲ **Adoption**
For a few families, adoption
becomes a life's mission. Joanne
and Scott Nuzum always wanted a
large family. Their son Danny has
29 adopted brothers and sisters,
most of them with special needs.
The Nuzums extended their home
four times to fit them all in.

Adoption today

Today, governments control
adoption to stop bad things
happening to children. They
also organize foster parents,
who care for children until
they can return to their
birth parents or find new
parents who will adopt
them. Strict rules aim to
make sure that adopted and
fostered children are safe,
happy and well matched to
their new families.

Until 20th-century
laws stopped them,
parents could adopt
children to use as
unpaid workers

15

Extended Families

HOW BIG IS YOUR FAMILY? Four, five people maybe? What about if you include aunts, nephews, grandparents and the rest? The sort of crowd that gathers for a wedding. You'll rapidly run out of fingers. This "extended family" including every living relation can easily number 50 or more.

Western ▲
This group from Indiana is an extended family typical of Western cultures. Colour-coded shirts indicate immediate family members. Great Grandma is central.

Inuit ▼
Like us, Arctic people have words for male and female relatives, such as aunts and uncles. They separate close family relatives, such as sisters, from distant ones, such as cousins.

Iroquois ▲
These Native American people trace their families much as we do. However, an Iroquois would call her mother's sister "Mum" and her father's brother "Dad". Their children are her brothers and sisters. People in south India use a similar system.

With so many relatives, we need words like "cousin" to figure out who's who. People from different continents identify family members very differently. Hawaiians, for instance, call an aunt "Mum". Cousins are either "brothers" or "sisters".

Tracing an extended family can be like untangling a knotted ball of wool

Counting cousins

Anthropologists (scientists who study people) record different family structures. Though they argue about how to classify extended families, most agree there are six or seven kinds. Some of them are explained here. And if understanding your own family is enough of a challenge, take a look at the family tree on page 44.

Would You Believe...?

Just call me confused

The Chiricahua language spoken by some Apache people is bafflingly short on relatives' names. Just one word, *shideedee*, means aunt, uncle, great aunt, great uncle, nephew and niece. Another word, *shinale*, can mean grandma, grandson or granddaughter!

Sudanese ▲

The people of Sudan in Africa have perhaps the most complicated family structures of all. Almost every relationship in a family has a different name. Some are impossible to translate into English. There are eight words just for "cousin".

▼ Nepalese

In Nepal, family members use different words for relatives of different ages. For example, the little girl in the middle of this picture does not have just one word for "brother". She calls her older brother her "*dai*" and the younger ones her "*bhais*".

Families,
Friends or Thieves?

A SECRET SOCIETY IS AN EXCITING way to tie friends together with a bond that each swears never to break. Some of us really never do. Pledges we make in the playground can help us to stay in touch with childhood friends all our lives.

A secret oath – with a penalty for breaking it – is not just a classroom fad. Powerful criminal organizations, such as the Mafia, use the same methods to keep members loyal to what they often call "the family".

Ancient practice
In the Middle Ages, members of craft guilds promised to keep secret the skills they shared. Modern clubs such as the Freemasons imitate the guilds' brotherhood ties.

The Mafia ▲
In the 1972 movie *The Godfather*, Marlon Brando plays the head of a New York crime family. The story and characters are based on the Mafia. This secret criminal society began in 19th-century Sicily. Members who emigrated to the USA took the society with them and gained wealth and power through drugs, blackmail and gun sales.

Would You Believe . . . ?
Scarface and family
A crime family led by Al "Scarface" Capone controlled 1920s Chicago and even the city's mayor. Capone's power so terrified his victims that no-one would give evidence against him. When he was finally jailed, it was for not paying his income tax.

◄ Freemasons
In Britain alone, 300,000 men belong to the Freemasons, having made pledges in an initiation process. Members claim it is a brotherhood that does charitable work. But others say the favours members do for each other are at best unfair, and at worst illegal.

A vow of silence protects Mafia secrets, and members are more loyal to their criminal brothers than to their real families

Criminal clubs, such as the Mafia and Yakuza, protect members from the police and government. They become more powerful than both, using bribes and threats to run whole cities.

Part of the family

Gang members benefit because their business rivals dare not oppose them. But they can pay a terrible price for this advantage. If they step out of line or refuse to help a brother, family justice is swift and deadly.

Yakuza families ▲▶
Whole-body tattoos are the trademark of the Yakuza "families" in Japan, which are responsible for much of Japan's crime. Yakuza members carry out one-third of the country's murders and two-thirds of all blackmail. The badges above are the signs of the four biggest Yakuza gangs.

What's in a Name?

PLENTY! NAMES TELL THE world not only who we are, but also who our ancestors were. Nobody was more sure of the importance of a name than the Ancient Egyptians. They believed that destroying a person's name destroyed all memory of them – someone without a name had never existed.

Our ancestors took names in many ways – from where they lived (Hill), what they did (Brewer), an ability (Strong) or the lack of one (Woodhead).

Slave names ▲
Black Americans sometimes change their family name to cast off memories of slavery. Slaves in America were renamed after their owners. This family of former slaves called the Wholes was photographed on a Georgia plantation in the 1900s.

Would You Believe . . . ?

Strange names
Many countries ban names that will embarrass a child. In 2008, a judge in New Zealand ordered a name change for a girl named "Talula does the Hula" from Hawaii. But another couple succeeded in naming their child "Number 16 Bus Shelter".

Common names ▲
The world's most common family name is Li, from China. More than 60 emperors of China had this family name, including 7th-century Emperor Taizong (above) from the Tang dynasty.

◀ **Family tree**
Trace your family back and you'll get a diagram that splits in two with each marriage. It's called a family tree because, with you on the trunk, it looks like a pattern of branches and twigs. Your family name is one branch. This is the family tree of German duke Ludwig von Herzog, produced in 1585.

▲ Named after Dad

Many family names come from the given name of the father. Williamson, for example, means "Son of William". Names formed in this way are called patronymics. Russian people have these as well as family names and given names.

Too good to use ▶

Native American tribal elders gave children names based on dreams or visions, but it was bad manners to use these personal names in conversation. Nicknames were used instead. This Sioux chief's name is Strike with Nose.

Families without names

Names haven't always identified ancestors. Chinese family names are perhaps the oldest. They began 4,700 years ago when Emperor Huang Ti gave his 12 sons different names. They passed these on to their children. Most Japanese people managed without family names until the 19th century. Even today, Tibetan people have two given names and no family name.

After his team won the FA Cup in 1965, a football fan named his child after all 11 players

Ghee and honey

◀ Naming ceremony

Giving a child a name is an important ceremony in most religions. This Hindu couple is naming a daughter in a ceremony called Namakarana. The father is giving his baby honey and ghee (clarified butter) on a ring and whispering her name in her ear.

21

Two Mums
or two Dads!

MUMS AND DADS DON'T come just in ones or twos. Some parents are polygamous – they have more than one partner. Extra wives are rare and extra husbands rarer still, and both are against the law in many places. But communes, where parents share partnerships and children, are not so unusual.

▲ **Extra husbands**
In the *Mahbharata*, a 3,000-year-old Indian epic tale, Princess Draupadi takes five princes as her husbands. Even when this tale was written, a woman with many husbands was shocking. In later centuries it was rare, except where men greatly outnumbered women.

In some Muslim countries today, a man can marry several wives – if the first wife agrees. Few men do, partly because big families are costly. Not many women have two husbands, though in Asia's Himalayas, a woman sometimes married two brothers to keep their land in one family.

▼ **Hippy communes**
In the 1960s, many hippies rejected "square" ideas of marriage and joined communes, such as California's Hog Farm. The idea was to share everything, including children, as one big family. In practice, men shared the women and the women shared the housework.

▶ Oneida community
Founded in Oneida, New York, in 1848, this Christian commune soon grew to 300 members. Their group marriage and shared child care caused outrage. It closed in 1881 and Oneida is now a cutlery company!

Large happy families

In communes, several parents care for all the children. In the 19th century, people formed communes such as the Oneida community, for political or religious reasons. In the 1960s, hippies made communes fashionable again, but not officially, because European and US laws restrict marriages to two people.

● ● ● ● ● ● ● ● ● ● ● ● ● ● ● ● ● ● ● ●

Nezahualpilli, Aztec ruler of the Mexican city of Texcoco, claimed he had more than 2,000 wives

▼ Two mums
This Muslim family from Xingiang Province in China has two mums and a dad. The Qu'ran, the Muslim holy book, allows men up to four wives. When the Qu'ran was written, in the 7th century, this seemed like a restriction because wealthy men had many more wives.

23

Sons or Daughters?

FOR PREGNANT MUMS, THE chances of having a boy or a girl are similar to those when you toss a coin. Each sex is equally likely. Yet if families could choose to have sons or daughters, there would be far more boys than girls. Want to know why? Ask a cave man.

Would You Believe . . . .?

Roman children
The Ancient Romans favoured boys, but Roman law obliged families to raise the first-born girl. According to a Roman proverb, "Every father, including a poor one, will raise a son, but even a rich man will abandon a daughter."

When men died, they passed on everything to their sons. They passed on their family names through their sons too. Daughters took on the name of their husband's family when they got married.

Mammoth hunt
Boys are bigger and stronger than girls, and when a family's survival depended on hunting or warfare, it celebrated the birth of a son. Later, as hunting gave way to farming and industry, men still wanted sons – to inherit their wealth and power.

▼ **Single-child policy**
China's schools echo with boys' voices. A 1980 law limiting children to one per family led to there being many more boys than girls. Now there are more than 13 men for each 10 women in rural areas.

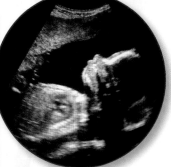

▲ **Baby scan**
Ultrasound scans before birth (above) show a baby's sex and show if he or she is free of any family diseases the parents may carry. Such parents can now also test their eggs before starting a "test-tube" pregnancy.

◀ The king wants a son!
English laws introduced in the 11th century gave family wealth to the first-born son on his father's death. The king's son got the crown too. So Henry VIII divorced one wife and executed another before the third, Jane Seymour, gave him a son.

Somali girl wearing silver and artificial amber beads as part of her dowry

Many parents without pensions believe that their sons will look after them when they are too old and tired to work

● ● ● ● ● ● ● ● ● ● ●

Doomed daughters

Ancient Greeks and Romans exposed unwanted female children to die of cold. Even when these murders were outlawed, more daughters died of neglect than sons. Killing or neglecting children is a crime everywhere today, but some parents decide to keep only sons.

Dowries ▶

Daughters are costly for families in areas where there is a custom of dowries. These are gifts from a bride's family to her husband. This Somali woman is wearing part of her dowry – a valuable necklace. For some brides, a trousseau of clothes and linen is a version of the dowry tradition.

25

Clay ancestor sculptures from the 2nd century

Living Together

Living with the dead ▲
If you believe that death is a journey into another life, having dead ancestors at home may seem OK. People as far apart as Scotland, Cyprus and Central America had a tomb under the floor. These figures decorated one in Mexico.

HUMANS LIKE COMPANY. We share our homes with parents or kids, often with a pet or two. Some families go much further. They move in with a whole farmyard of animals – or even their dead ancestors.

House size makes less difference than custom. In places where it's traditional for whole families to live together, three or more generations may share tiny, cramped homes. But in modern Britain, old people often prefer living on their own, even if their children have a spare room in which they could stay.

Where housing is costly, it's not unusual for four generations to share a home

◀ **All part of the family**
This present-day family from Mongolia, Central Asia, has brought new-born lambs into their yurt (tent home) to protect them from the weather. This was common everywhere in the past: the family home doubled as a barn or stable for the livestock.

Change of use

Changing customs and fashions affect not only who crams into the family home, but what we all choose to do there. One hundred years ago, people's homes were the centre of their lives and leisure. Today, though, we are more likely to use our homes just as bases for eating, sleeping and washing before going out to get on with busy independent lives elsewhere.

Boomerang kids ▲

Unemployment and the soaring cost of housing mean that more and more kids move back home after college. Half of university students now say they expect to live at home after graduation.

Would You Believe . . . . ?

Animal heating
Keeping animals in the home isn't just about raising them successfully. Animals can take the place of central heating. A cow produces about 1 kilowatt of heat – as much as a small radiator – and a sow with piglets, nearly half this.

▲ Victorian family

In 19th-century English towns, families used the home to eat most of their meals together, to share crafts and entertain each other, all under the watchful eye of the *paterfamilias* (family dad). Only adults led independent lives outside the home.

▼ Eating alone

Eating together used to be a twice-daily routine, but when family members keep different schedules, most of us end up eating alone. Just one in 20 families now eats together around a dining table, and one-third use it only for Christmas and birthdays.

Families Doing Things Together

WHAT SHALL WE DO TODAY? Where shall we go on holiday? These are modern questions. Not long ago, only families with slaves or servants could regularly spare the time to relax together. For others, festivals such as Christmas and Easter provided the only times they could meet, celebrate and play.

Increasing wealth gave people more time together and technology gave them new things to do. The 19th-century invention of railways provided cheap transport, making more family holidays possible. In the 20th century, people had movies, radio and TV to share.

▲ **Special celebrations**
Although Christians began celebrating Christmas around 350 CE, it became an occasion for a big family gathering only in the 19th century. Even then, it was easier for wealthy families to enjoy it – the servant girl on the left of this picture isn't spending Christmas with *her* family.

Summer holidays ▲
Holidays with white-knuckle rides and ice-cream weren't possible until 20th-century laws gave workers paid time off. Before that, factory workers had just a week's unpaid break. Many families could afford only to go to the country to pick fruit.

Performing together

Performing together helps a family to harmonize – even if they fight when they are out of the spotlight! In music, the Jonas Brothers continue a tradition that goes back to the Jacksons and beyond, and big-top family acts are as old as circus itself.

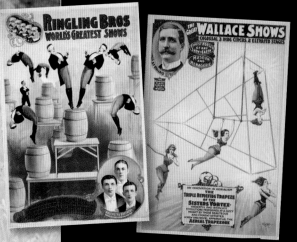

Circus families ▲
Circus stars start training almost as soon as they can walk, so it's hardly surprising that they perform with the parents who taught them. Family teams are especially suitable for the trapeze – the smallest family members do the flying and the strongest catch them.

Old and new

Today, technology shapes what we do together. Even on holiday we can stay in touch with our friends and family by text or phone. But some family pastimes just don't change. We enjoy watching sports matches or going shopping much as our grandparents did.

▲ Mushroom picking
A family outing to collect mushrooms is an autumn tradition in Europe, Japan and the USA. Parents pass on identification tips because mistakes can make the difference between dinner and death.

● ● ● ● ● ● ● ● ● ● ● ● ● ● ● ● ●

Victorian servants worked every day – but had Mothers' Day off to spend with their families

Would You Believe . . . ?

Trying for a team
Jokes about big families and sports teams didn't make the Rodriguez family laugh. All 14 picked crops for a living in 1960s Texas. Workers relaxed by playing baseball. The Rodriguez family – with six sons and six daughters – had a team and substitutes!

Working Together

Would You Believe . . . ?

Minimum wages
Sweatshop labour employs whole families at poverty wages. New York families making paper flowers in 1911 could make 150 in an hour. This earned them just a dollar a day. Today, South Asian sweatshops making trainers and footballs pay little better.

Junior miners ▲
Sons followed their fathers down mines to learn coal mining skills. This boy coupled coal trucks in a Tennessee mine in 1910. Thirty years passed before laws banned children from dangerous jobs.

IN THE PAST, families who lived together often worked together. By watching their parents, children learned useful skills – simple ones at first, then harder tasks. By the time they were teenagers, they worked as fast as their parents – or faster.

Every family member helped, even the youngest. On farms, toddlers scared birds while their parents hoed. In towns, 3-year-olds sorted the straw their parents plaited into hats. A 1720 visitor to a weaver's house noted with approval that the whole family was busy "from the youngest to the oldest".

Bringing in the harvest ▼
Crops don't wait. They rot if they are not picked, so at harvest time, the whole family helps. This picture was taken in 1944, in County Maine, USA, but in country areas kids still take time out of school when there are potatoes to dig.

New York sweatshops ▲
European immigrants to the USA in the early 20th century arrived with no money. Crowded into tiny tenements (flats), families worked together at badly paid jobs such as shelling nuts. The work was nicknamed "sweated labour" and the tenements "sweatshops".

Watch and learn ▶
Skills can jump
generations. This boy
in Assam, northeast
India, is watching his
grandfather fishing. He
is learning something
that he will teach his
own grandchildren.

Family poverty

Children who worked
with their parents learnt useful skills, but family
working had a darker side. Everybody lent a
hand because without the children, the family
would starve. Home work and farm work
were badly paid, and families survived only by
working every hour of daylight.

**US labour laws don't protect
children on family farms,
who still do dangerous work**

Working family ▼
Cows need milking
twice a day, so this farm
family share the chore of
filling buckets. They do
it by hand because they
are Amish, a religious
group that rejects
mechanical aids.

Ice fishing ▲
For the Inuit people
of the Arctic, fishing
wasn't a hobby but
an essential skill
that fathers taught
sons. Most Inuit now
shop for food, but the
tradition continues.

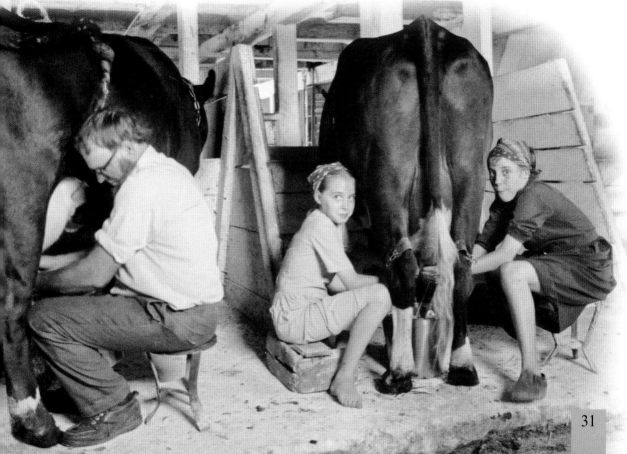

Who's in Charge?

IT'S AN ORDER YOU DARE NOT disobey: "You do it NOW because I say so, and I'm your father!" Dads can lay down the law because, even today, men control most families. It's fathers who give the family its name. And until recently, everything a family owned belonged to the father.

Societies in which men are in charge are called patriarchal, but they are not the only type of society. A few places in the world have matriarchal families. In these, children take their mum's name and women own all the property.

Child power

Some parents now share authority, and children may have a say in family decisions. A century ago, children were little more than their father's property. But since the 1970s, campaigners for children's rights have ensured that they are respected and treated as individuals.

The matriarch ▲
The Mosuo people of Lake Lugo in China live in one of the few societies where women are in charge. It is known as "the Women's Kingdom". There, mums head families – and also do most of the work.

The patriarch ▼
The tradition of the father controlling everything is very old. Ancient Greece is famous as a democracy. Everyone shared political decisions – if they were men. Women didn't count, in politics or at home.

Would You Believe . . . ? Would You Believe . . . ?

Kids in control
In medieval Europe, children controlled the family and told their parents what to do – but only on one day of the year. At the Feast of Fools, on 1 January, everyone swapped places. A peasant child became "boy bishop" for the day.

"Why would you want a marriage licence to handcuff yourself?" – a Mosuo woman from China talking about her society's woman-centred families

Children's rights ▶
In some countries, laws allow children unhappy with their parents' care and decisions to be emancipated (declared independent adults). Hollywood actress Drew Barrymore had a wild childhood and successfully applied for emancipation at 15 years old.

DREW BARRYMORE

Drew Barrymore's star on the Hollywood Walk of Fame

Sharing ▲
Women who ask that chores and decisions in family life – and everything else in the home – are shared, often find that what they get isn't quite what they had wanted. Though dads help with looking after children, and both partners go to work, research shows that women still end up doing most of the housework.

Mums in charge

In the late 19th century, women won more influence in family decisions as part of a wider campaign for women's rights. Known as the Suffragettes, the campaigners also won women the right to vote and have equal access to education. Later, the feminist movement of the 1960s and 70s helped mothers to demand – and get – a more equal share of family power.

Nanny
Knows Best

◀ **Au-pairs**
Many parents employ au-pairs, usually young foreign women, to help with the kids. *Au-pair* is French for "as equal", and the women are supposed to be just that in the family.

RICH PARENTS OF THE PAST WHO were too busy, lazy or squeamish to raise a family found the perfect solution: nannies. These mums-for-hire looked after children so that their real parents didn't have to.

Nurses raised children even in Ancient Egypt, 3,300 years ago, but the job of nanny is newer. It began around 1800. A growing population meant more young women were looking for work. And more parents than ever before were rich enough to hire them.

Milk brothers ▲
There have been wet-nurses (women who feed babies who are not their own) since ancient times. In Muslim societies, the children are milk-brothers and sisters. They may not marry and are free of the rules separating men and women of different families.

Animal nannies ▶
In a 20th-century story by Edgar Rice Burroughs, African apes raise a human child. He grows into Tarzan the ape man, who can talk to all the animals. In real life, it's extremely rare for animals to raise human children successfully.

Wet-nurses ▲
French king Louis XIV is shown here with a wet-nurse. Women whose own children may have died breast-fed children of wealthy families before bottle feeding became safe a century ago.

Would You Believe . . . ?
Russian wolf nannies
In 2007, in a story remarkably like that of Romulus and Remus (see page 14), police rescued a boy who had been raised by wolves in a forest in central Russia. The "wolf-boy" snarled and bit, could not speak and ate like an animal.

Nanny in charge
Wealthy 19th-century European families handed over almost every bit of child care to nannies. Indeed, some parents saw their children only briefly, when they were presented after tea by a uniformed nanny.

◄ Starched nannies
Nannies began to dress in a special way, differently from other servants, around 1850. Their starched uniform was similar to that of Victorian nurses. Both outfits gave protection against smells and spills.

Nannies' close contact with the family made them the most powerful servants in a house

Today, parents want a bigger part in their children's lives and few can afford full-time servants. Many make do with almost-nannies, such as au-pairs. Real nannies still push prams in swanky parts of town, but without uniforms they are hard to spot!

Mary Poppins ►
Nannies really were as strict as the storybook kind, such as Mary Poppins. As her employer says in the 1964 movie, "Nanny must be a general: tradition, discipline and rule ... without them you have a ghastly mess."

Kids or Parents?

BEING A MUM OR DAD IS something most of us do only when we're adults. But for a few unlucky children, the duty of running a family comes while they are still growing up. Children have to look after their families when war or AIDS takes away their parents. Poverty and sickness can force parents and children to swap roles too.

▼ **Earning their keep**
These American kids from 1910 lived in a former chicken house while they picked fruit to keep their family afloat. This would be illegal today, but many poor US families need the money their children earned in the holidays.

▼ **Looking after older folk**
Adult children may be happy to look after Gran or ageing Mum, but for teenagers it can be a huge responsibility. Carer-kids have to grow up quickly, can lose touch with friends and often end up missing out on school and college.

Of course, it's nothing new for children to have to earn wages or care for brothers and sisters or older people in the family. What *is* new is the number of kids who have to do it now. And the number of reasons for these upside-down families is growing.

Taking care of brothers and sisters

In China alone, more than 58 million kids have been left behind by their parents when they went to seek work and higher wages in distant cities. And in Africa, 12 million children have lost one or both parents to AIDS. Many of these abandoned kids are now bringing up their younger brothers and sisters.

▲ **Baby-sitting**
Today it's a way for teenagers to earn some cash, but in the past, baby-sitting was an unpaid chore and a way for young girls to learn about parenting skills. This painting of 1871 shows a French girl looking after her younger brother.

More than half of China's left-behind children have to look after themselves

AIDS destroying families ▶
In parts of Africa, so many parents die of AIDS that one in ten families is cared for by a child like this girl from Tanzania. Kids as young as eight are forced to raise their brothers and sisters, often after caring for dying parents.

37

Family Substitutes

NOTHING BEATS THE SENSE OF belonging that you get from being part of a family – but a school, gang or club can come close. Those who join these special groups sometimes describe them as families and call each other "brother" or "sister". The bonds and friendships they form can be as strong as any family tie.

▲ **Street families**
There is constant danger for street children like these newspaper sellers from early-20th-century New Jersey. So they quickly learn to stick together like brothers and defend each other. Newsboys each had their own pitch (selling spot) and united to fight off intruders.

▲ **Kibbutzim**
First set up in Palestine in 1909, kibbutzim were Jewish communes where children studied and lived together. Growing up in a kibbutz built up kids' Jewish brotherhood and encouraged them to defend their Israeli state.

- Medieval parents understood about strong bonds and used them to form alliances between their families.
- In Japan and across Europe, noblemen sent their sons away from home to join households of other great families. Growing up as pages and squires (trainee knights) they became loyal to their substitute families.

Schools and gangs can exclude outsiders with speech. Secret words or even a whole language sound like nonsense to anyone not in the club.

He's my brother
Modern groups inspire the same loyalty as those of the past. In a street gang or warrior school, loyalty ensures that each member defends and protects his "brother".

◀ **Boarding school**
An "old school tie" is not just a necktie belonging to ex-boarding-school boys. It is also the friendship that *ties* them together after they leave school. Harry Potter's Hogwarts is based on 19th-century British schools for children whose parents were abroad governing the country's vast empire.

Martial arts school ▼
Schools that educate children in the art of war often have harsh conditions, strict discipline and make students work hard. Pupils grow closer because they endure the pain and danger together. Here, kids at Shaolin Temple Wushu school in China have got up early for vigorous morning exercise.

Would You Believe . . . ?

Hunger bonding
In the warrior-schools of Ancient Greece, hunger bound classes together. Their meals were so tiny that they were forced to steal food. Students were whipped if they were caught – not for thieving, but for being too stupid to avoid discovery.

It's in your Genes

Would You Believe . . . ? Would You Believe . . . ?

Peas and bees
The scientist who discovered how genes work was 19th-century Austrian monk Gregor Mendel. He did it by growing 29,000 pea plants. Repeating his work with bees, he bred only a vicious stinger, and scientists ignored his breakthrough for 50 years.

A FAMILY ALBUM IS LIKE a mirror. Look in yours and you will see that your parents once looked much as you do now. Family members are alike because parents pass their genes on to their children. Genes are natural codes for features such as hair and eye colour. They are part of a tiny, twisting rope of DNA, which contains the "instructions" for our cells and is almost everywhere in our bodies.

We get half our genes from each parent, which is why relations may say, "He's got his mum's mouth and his dad's eyes." Brothers and sisters are not identical because the genes mix differently in each child.

Charles I, King of Spain, 1500–1558

Philippe IV
1605–1665

Leopold I
1640–1705

Charles II
1661–1700

◀▲ Inbreeding and genetic diseases
Genes can go wrong, leading to genetic diseases, which parents pass on to their children. This is more likely when people "inbreed" (marry relations), so in many places marriage between relatives closer than first cousin is illegal. The Hapsburgs, one of Europe's royal families, ignored such rules, and Charles I's descendants all inherited his deformed jaw. Genetic disease killed his great, great, great grandson Charles II ("Charles the Cursed").

Baffling genes

The mixture of genes from parents can sometimes have puzzling results. Parents with different coloured skin may have a black son and a white daughter. Genes can also jump generations. Kids with two brown-eyed parents, for example, usually have brown eyes. But they *may* have blue eyes if two of their grandparents are blue-eyed.

Identical twins ▶
A mum has identical twins when the egg inside her grows into two babies instead of one. "Identical" twins have exactly the same genes, but they are never quite the same. They have different fingerprints, for example.

▲ Ear-wax
Things we inherit from our parents usually rely on several genes, but just one gene controls ear-wax. Africans and Europeans have one form, which makes their wax moist. A different form makes everyone else's wax dry.

The Spanish royal line of the Hapsburgs died out because they married each other to "keep the blood pure"

● ● ● ● ● ● ● ● ● ● ● ● ● ● ● ● ● ●

Four generations ▶
Genes don't affect just details such as the colour of your hair, eyes and skin. Through her genes, the great grandmother in this picture will have handed on to her son, her granddaughter and her great grandchildren things like her height, her good temper and her resistance to some diseases.

41

A Stylish Farewell

King Tut ▲
This gold mask of Egypt's pharaoh Tutankhamun covered his face in his tomb. Ancient Egyptians preserved the bodies of the dead because they believed that decay prevented them from living again in the afterlife.

WHETHER WE are rich or poor, famous or humble, family life always finishes the same way. Everyone ends up boxed up and buried, or burned in a cremation. In the past, funerals had more variety. Egyptians preserved their dead relations as mummies. Where soil and fuel were short, people fed corpses to birds or ants.

Jazz funeral ▲
Traditions of French brass bands and African-American slave music come together in New Orleans jazz funerals. The musicians play sad tunes as they follow the coffin, but break into a livelier rhythm once the burial is over.

Burial at sea ▼
Dead sailors are "buried" at sea – slipped overboard in a weighted coffin. On sailing battleships in the past, the corpse was sewn into a sail with a cannonball at each end. By tradition, the last stitch went between the nostrils as a final check for signs of life.

▲ **Pan de muerto**

◄ **Day of the Dead**
On 2 November each year, people in Mexico celebrate the Day of the Dead, when they honour their dead ancestors. They hold graveside parties and leave offerings of food and drink. Bakers produce food such as marzipan skulls and *pan de muerto* (dead bread).

Some funeral customs sound grisly, but only if we don't think of death as a natural end to life. Graves aren't scary if you party round them every year, or if you believe, as Egyptians did, that they lead to another life.

In the traditional "sky burials" of frozen Tibet, birds of prey feed on the bodies of the dead, which are left exposed in sacred places

Fantasy coffin ▼
Want to be buried in a running shoe, in a giant hot-dog or in a fish like this? Then you'd better die in Ghana, west Africa. For the last 50 years, there has been a tradition in the capital, Accra, of elaborate, decorated coffins. The best cost a year's wages.

Coffin of a fisherman

Noisy send-off
Funerals can be fun, once you have wiped the tears from your eyes. They bring together far-flung families, and in many parts of the world, such as New Orleans, they turn into noisy occasions to celebrate the life of a relative.

Balinese funeral ▲
On the Indonesian island of Bali, a cremation is a joyous celebration that frees a dead person's spirit to come to life again. Bodies of wealthy people burn inside costly statues.

Would You Believe . . . ? Would You Believe . . . ?

Go out with a bang
Cremation is a fiery way to leave the world, but it's not very green. Though bodies contain as much fuel as 6 litres (13 pints) of petrol, they need more to burn completely. The extra fuel needed could power a car for more than 560 kilometres (350 miles).

Understand your Family Tree

IF THIS BOOK INTERESTED YOU – and it must have done, if you've read this far – you may want to find out more about where you fit into your family. The tree below should help. Once you've got your brain around it, try sketching your own, with real names under the squares and circles and photos inside. The links opposite will help you get started.

Would You Believe . . . . ?

World's tallest family tree
In 2008, scientists extracted genes from bones found in a cave in Germany. They matched the genes of two men living nearby. This proved the cave-dwellers were ancestors of both men – putting them both on a family tree 120 generations long.

▼ **Who's really who?**
Do you know the difference between a great aunt and a first cousin once removed? Families are baffling, but a family tree shows who's who. The brown bands on this one show who is in each generation – on the same "step" down from an ancestor.

Family tree

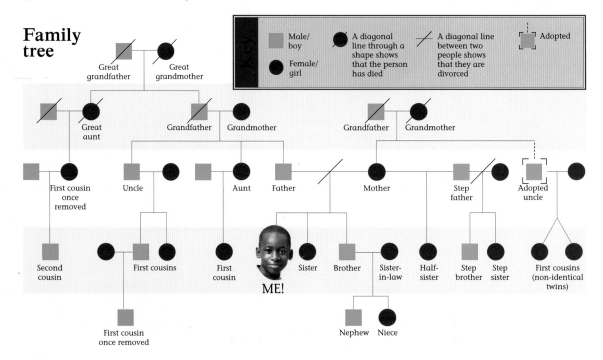

Key

■ Male/boy	⊘ A diagonal line through a shape shows that the person has died	╱ A diagonal line between two people shows that they are divorced	⬚ Adopted
● Female/girl		

Great grandfather — Great grandmother

Great aunt — Grandfather — Grandmother — Grandfather — Grandmother

First cousin once removed — Uncle — Aunt — Father — Mother — Step father — Adopted uncle

Second cousin — First cousins — First cousin — ME! — Sister — Brother — Sister-in-law — Half-sister — Step brother — Step sister — First cousins (non-identical twins)

First cousin once removed

Nephew — Niece